Musings
of a
Preacher's Son

NICHOLAS A. VERONIS

ISBN 978-1-63525-262-0 (Paperback)
ISBN 978-1-63525-263-7 (Digital)

Christian Faith Publishing, Inc.
296 Chestnut Street
Meadville, PA 16335
www.christianfaithpublishing.com

Printed in the United States of America

To the Glory of God

Contents

A Dog

The greatest creature of God's fold
Providing love when life is cold
Always forgiving and kind
And a savior to the blind

Eager to run even faster
When called to come by his master
Even when spurned and neglected
His forgiveness is perfected

A noble and incomparable friend
And a companion up until the end
A dog always sees only the best
And feels honored to join in your quest

When he grows older and slow
His love does not cease to glow
Although his time to sleep is near
His spirit and conscience are clear

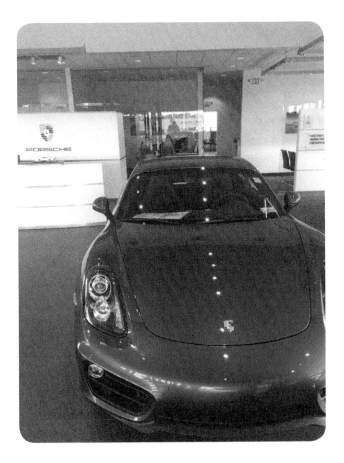

Advertising

Oh, how it preoccupies the sight and muddles the mind
Portraying mere things as the ultimate find
Promising salvation which will enhance your life
And bring you happiness and a state free of strife

Tempting you to spend on that which you do not need
It makes you restless, discontent, and unable to read
It can possess one's being from prayer and reflection
And lead a person to ignore much-needed confession

Once obtained, it always results in disappointment
When you realize it is incapable of bringing true ointment
Those who do not have it lust after it more
In the hopes that working harder will get them that score

In the end one again finds out it was just ashes and dust
When you discover that which shone brightly, mere flashes then rust
Be cautious for the snake disguised in slippery talk and bright lights
For it will choke and smother you from seeing that which is right

Always be on guard for what really matters
Love people, not things as you ascend John's ladder.

Ambition

It drives a person to lead
And inspires one to succeed
It can result in progress
Or stifle change like Congress

If buttressed by faith and contemplation
It suppresses regret and consternation
If abused by those who are selfish and greedy
It leads to excess and takes from the needy

All leaders possess the trait
And use it to replicate the great
Put forth in moderation it betters our existence
But uncontrolled it leads to narcissistic persistence

So beware of this intoxicating power
It can lead to arrogance and cause others to cower
Although used to motivate the lazy
It can blind and make some people crazy

A Mother

The person who is there to protect your back
When life presents challenges that are stacked
A guiding light who is thinking of you
And believes you are full of strength and true

The one who was there when you first appeared
In a world of chaos with much fear
She held you tight and kept you warm
From unfamiliar faces and the storm

The person who knows you can be more
And gives you truth and wisdom to store
Her unspoken prayers help keep you from strife
To reinforce and fortify your life

A good mother is more precious than treasure
The ultimate gift from God without measure
So give thanks and honor to your mother on this special day
Without such an influence, you would be lost in many ways

Anger

A feeling that disturbs one's peace of mind
And makes a person sullen and unkind
Tempting one to say things which he will long regret
And committing actions which he may not forget

A passion controlled by the spiritually wise
It is often inflamed by a secular lie.
Commonly it emanates from enemies and differences
But also can be found among lovers and mistresses.

Causing men to say things which will not be forgotten
It leads to resentment and conditions most rotten.
Forgiveness is the only balm to ease the state
When irrational men become ungodly and irate.

Although not unique to either young or old
It seems life's experiences mellow the cold.
Allowing the enraged man to regain his composure
And restore a positive mood to bring about closure.

Charisma

A power possessed by very few
A force of nature innate and on cue
Mesmerizing the masses and the envy of all
The persona within which can conquer the fall

Attractive and keen it is hard to hide
When the person speaks boldly and rides on the tide
Unforgettable and vivacious, it meets every challenge
And holds out hope for the meek and the weak

Bold, brave, and confident, it arouses the masses
To meet every challenge with rose colored glasses
Few have what it takes to weather the storm
But its eternal optimism holds out hope for the norm

Let charisma prevail when evil is caught
So that hope is presented for that which is bought
Let the people rejoice over the one who remains
Providing comfort and charm to the clinically insane

Compassion

We are born naked with no human fare
With no clothes, no money, no earthly care.
If blessed with good parents we are taught to love all
To emulate God's word and to follow his call.

We see Jesus in all people and must heed his command
That whomever you assist will always be in demand.
He has taught us to help the least of our brother
In return he will lift us up like his mother.

Be kind, true, and honorable when pursuing your call
For tomorrow may bring hardship which could lead to us all.
Live in the present and be conscious of your thoughts
And you will be more likely to overcome your faults.

Share all you have with those who do not
And the Lord will reward you with all his lot.
Do not hoard your money and build bigger barns
For tomorrow He may call you to vacate the farm.

Contentment

A feeling of being which is elusive
As one searches for things that are intrusive
Never finding that perfect match
Or settling on that certain catch

Knowing full well that it is found within
Yet seeking fashion or a bottle of gin
Those who obtain it find the ultimate high
Finding meaning and happiness before they die

Sought by holy men and the wise
Who seek to help those who despise
It leads to healthy self-esteem
Releasing one's loftier dreams

Once obtained it frees the soul
Helping one achieve his goal
It allows a person's guilt to be assuaged
Rewarding the mind with a heavenly stage

Death

Always lurking when least expected
Part of life which is unprotected.
Some fear it with loathing and contempt
While others show their strength and repent.

For some it comes with misery and doubt
While others succumb with faith, so stout.
To the young it is rare and unspoken
To the old it is real and unbroken.

When the priest comes to offer Holy Communion
The faithful know that it is time for the union.
The children grieve and the widow is in all black
As somber men carry a coffin from the back.

The deceased is eulogized with the highest acclaim
As his friends and family sing praises to his name.
Although he will be missed by a few friends and his clan
The world moves forward with God's eternal plan.

Demons

Spewing forth from the bowels of hell
Demons assail the humble priest ringing a church bell.
Never content with those whose inner peace is intact
They fight hard to poison those with whom God has a pact.

Knowing that men are quite vulnerable and weak
They seek to possess both the strong and the meek.
Using the tools of their trade, most notably
greed, power and passion
They achieve their desired result in most clever fashion.

The demons love prejudice and hate filled thought
And revel when people of different creeds and colors have fought.
Their power is quite evident in our world at the present
As they go to great liberty to create fearful resentment.

Although they temporarily succeed with those who have fear
Their influence wanes when God's people draw near.
Their ultimate goal is suffering, death and a downward flight
Yet we know that the Lord's resurrection rescues us from that plight.

Faith

Some perceive it with all their might
Others ignore it in plain sight.
To some it is resolute
Bringing wisdom so astute

It leads some to share their lives
To render compassion and tithes
It compels some to commit to a fast
While others use it to reverse their past

It stirs and inspires the soul
Giving one purpose and a goal
It makes leaders selfless and benign
Putting holiness in charge of time

It can lead to transformation
And result in sweet salvation
Those who embrace and confess it
Will be blessed with a divine fit

Fleeting Life

Oh, life, how rapidly you pass
Quietly, like a solemn mass.
Love and laughter we have had
Far more good than bad.

Caring parents passing on their faith
Giving hope and comfort to our fallen race.
Forget not to enjoy the finer things in life
Like sons and daughters and a loving wife.

Yet time is so fleeting that it waits for no man's role
And has a way of humbling those who disregard its toll.
Giving strength to the young and wisdom to the old
Knowing that in time we all return to the same fold.

Let us not live in the future or dwell on the past
Seize instead the present so we do not miss the cast.
Life moves forward without stopping as the moments tick away
Hoping only that we use it in a most productive way.

As God has warned, we must always be on look
Our time to go is not recorded in any earthly book
For there may be little time for peace
Before He calls us to the great feast.

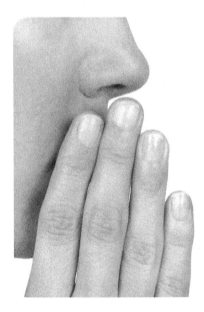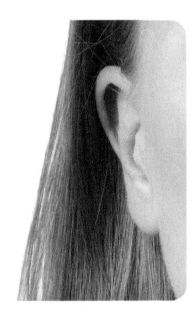

Gossip

Idle talk passed on without a care
By those who know well they should not dare.
Often unkind language meant to harm
And not put forth for goodwill or charm.

It can ruin the image of a noble fella
Or taint the innocence of a sweet bella.
Spread by vicious and simple minded people
Who have learned little under a church steeple.

The wise discuss ideas and knowledge
Some ignore the lessons of college.
They relish in passing on the mundane
Embellishing rumors they cannot contain.

Beware of people who are quick to leak
The secrets you share with those whom you speak.
Not meant for good and inspiration
It can result in condemnation.

Gratitude

A moment of reflection
To overcome dejection
An expression of thanks for all that is good
A gesture to God for life and parenthood

Seizing highs and lows in stride
To make the most of one's short ride
Realizing that things do not fulfill
But rather enslave a person's will

Missing out on the beauty of each day
By obsessing on issues that have no say
Focusing solely on that which glitters
Makes a person feel restless and bitter

Sadness remains for those who are blind
In failing to seek the ultimate find
Maintaining balance for true contentment
Will bring you gratitude, not resentment

Healing

A miracle of life often overlooked
Yet as potent as any force or book
Sent by the Lord to transform
The body to its purest form

A power of nature triggering hope
Bringing optimism greater than dope
A transformation of the soul
Curing itself with a new role

Emanating from our Lord
A being which is restored
Moving forward with new life
A renewed lease without strife

Gratitude to God for his mercy
Thankful for no more controversy
Realizing that good health is a gift
Which one can lose with alarming swift

Humility

A gift from God sometimes found in holy monasteries
Its source cannot be bought in exotic apothecaries.
Seldom possessed by czars and kings in opulent places
But often by servants and slaves with weathered faces.

Although some feel it is the product of the weak
It is innate to the spiritually strong and the meek.
For some men it is natural and true
Whiles others struggle without a clue.

It can balance the dangers of power and conceit
And nurture the soul with a feeling so complete.
The men who possess it find peace in their lives
While those it evades often have failure and hives.

It can be found in people of all social classes
But not always in pious self-righteous masses.
It attracts the wisdom of the sages
Absolving men from violent rages.

Its origin is found in the Holy One who came
To save us from our fallen nature and self-imposed fame.

Impulsiveness

Restlessness that is innate
Driving a person's daily fate
Never at rest in the mind
Looking for that unknown find

Inner peace which does not come
Turmoil that makes you numb
Seeking that rest to ease the pain
Tormenting the soul like a chain

Never happy with the present
Wanting to be omnipresent
Talking and dealing distracts the feeling
Yet life is full warp and unappealing

Some try to slow its manifestation
By silence and simple concentration
Living in the present is a good start
To ease its damage to the inner heart

Jealousy

A feeling emanating from human pride
Seldom found in any animal tribe
A sensation that stirs from the depth of one's being
It tastes like bile and smothers rational feeling.

Compelling good people to view with disdain
The achievements of those who do not complain.
Sometimes triggered by misguided love or lust
It can ruin those whose memories we trust.

Its passion frightens those victimized by its ire
And can lead to hatred and an unquenchable fire.
It has no logic and despises common sense
Causing one to erect an imaginary fence.

Although its origin has no reason or simple rationale
Its consequences result in treason and moods quite often foul.
Left uncontrolled it leads to misery and strife
And sometimes even causes the taking of human life.

Loneliness

A feeling of emptiness worse than death
Making one feel desperate and short of breath
Suffocating the spirit and the soul
It can lead to a loss of self-control

The lonely person seeks to ease the pain
By ingesting substances which do not sustain
Reeling from a life of hopeless isolation
Despite existing in a dense population

Thirsting for human love and affection
In meaningful relationships with connection
So common to the human race
It is more painful than disgrace

It should not be prevalent in a civilized nation
Where life and liberty lead to lofty expectations
With a helping hand and true introspection
Hope can be found within the resurrection

Character

The essence of one's being
Discovery and seeing
That which brings true happiness
Living a life of selflessness

Realizing that to be honest and true
Is greater than IQ and revenue
That which inspires a person
To be good and to take a stand

Controlled by a person's inner thoughts
Doing what is right despite the costs
Standing up to evil when it arises
Despite the consequences and surprises

Leading to selfless sacrifice
Resisting temptation and vice
Seeing the good in all around
Protecting nature which abounds

Not hoarding possessions and wanting more
Realizing that things are just a bore
Showing compassion to the downtrodden and weak
Not feeling superior because you can speak

Accepting that there is a power greater than you
That brings you divine peace which comes into view
Guided by your conscience which can keep you on track
Ensuring you live a life which is holy, not black

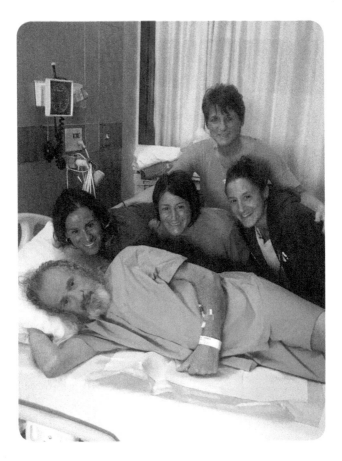

The Illness

It comes on in a flash
Stunning life with a crash
Your first instinct is denial
Then realism brings the trial

Life as you knew it is put on hold
As you grasp for miracles so bold
Spirituality becomes more real
As you realize the mundane is concealed

Loved ones are shocked to learn the dark news
And your friends react as though confused
They try to offer a positive stance
But their words of solace do not enhance

Time slows down as if lost to the mind
As mortality becomes so defined
The future is no longer a cause for concern
As the present becomes more precious, yet stern

You think back to all the joys you have had
Realizing that they have outweighed the bad
You are thankful for the good years God has given
Yet your soul yearns for hope and being forgiven

Although all people will face this inevitable time
When it comes, most recoil as if accused of a crime
No living being can escape its wrath
When our time to go crosses our path

For the Christian, there is the promise of tomorrow
When we will be reunited without this sorrow
We do not perish in vain or leave our loved ones in despair
For we believe in the promise of eternal life so fair

Lust

Obsessing the mind
It makes the sane blind.
Yet disguised as true love
It is not so divine.

For beauty allows the body to rule
Forsaking good sense and making one drool.
All reason is swallowed by the sensuous sight
Leading to actions which do not seem right.

Seen by God as a powerful vice
He allows free will in spite of the price.
Some fall for this passion before it abates
But the damage is done and subject to fate.

The wise flee from its grasp as soon as it rises
Knowing that to tempt it will lead to surprises.
So beware of this siren with golden hair
A serpent in heat which one should not dare.

Money

Sought by so many as the ultimate goal
It can obsess the mind and make the sane lose their role.
Never enough, it can lead to destruction
And make one think he can forgo reconstruction.

Used wisely and for good, it can transform the earth
But hoarded and praised it results in great mirth.
The right balance can lead to peace and posterity
Too much results in a false sense of security.

Preoccupied and possessed by the lure of the green
It can mesmerize the weak and fatten the lean.
Warned by God that it can blind the path to heaven
Making our bread tasteless and lacking sweet leaven.

So heed the warning of those who have gone before
Seeking riches solely for self will lead to nothing more.

Our Risen Lord

Born in a manger surrounded by beasts
Three kings came to praise him from the Far East
His mission was known to his father above
Yet misunderstood by the people he loved

His mother a virgin as holy as could be
He was raised by a carpenter close to the sea
Soon he embarked on his life as a teacher
A fisher of men, an itinerant preacher

Few people knew that he was the Messiah
The Pharisees looked on him as a pariah
Performing miracles and raising Lazarus from the dead
His influence and fame became even more widespread

Despite his power, he was as humble as a dove
Changing lives as he taught his disciples to love
He preached that the meek shall inherit the earth
And to love your enemies and those of low birth

He was soon betrayed by one of his own
Given to Pilate and tortured to the bone
To fulfill his Godly mission he was handed over to die
And crucified with two criminals on a hill near the sky

His body was pierced as he gasped his last breath
Those around him not knowing he'd soon conquer death
He was placed in a sealed off tomb of stone within
And in three days was resurrected to save us from sin

His legacy has lasted for two thousand years
Transforming lives with hope and less fear
We praise him today and rejoice on high
As we sing "Christ Is Risen" in joyous reply!

Peace

Some seek it through material things
Lusting silver and gold worn by kings.
Others hope to find it through pleasure
Feeling the more will be their measure.

Some search for it in fancy clothes or castles
Or knowledge resulting in bright-colored tassels.
Some yearn for it through power
As if it abodes in some lofty tower.

Some seek it through spirits or luxury cars
Unaware that it cannot be found in exotic bars.
The spiritually wise who possess the gift
Understand in time it is the ultimate lift.

Realizing that life is not always a ball
It is present in those who respond to the call.
Stirring from deep within the soul
It can save you from paying the ultimate toll.

Once obtained it provides a magnificent high
Far greater than anything money can buy.
Peace of mind is the state which we all seek
Often overlooked by the strong but seldom the meek.

For lest we forget
Life on earth is no more than a lease
A stairway to heaven and eternal peace.

Power

Emanating from within and strangling the mind
Making grown men irrational and often unkind.
It enraptures the brain and defiles the soul
Often hidden by beauty, it can blacken like coal.

It ignores moderation and forsakes common sense
Often leading to tragedy and situations most tense.
While beguiling the weak and oppressing the masses
It can forever enslave the lads and the lasses.

Feeding the ego and flaming the fire
It can lead to destruction and misplaced ire.
Where evil tempted good and let fate set it free.
Having come from a garden with a snake and a tree

Controlled and in check, it can be used for progress
But when volatile and in heat, it can be like Congress.
Employed by some to make the world a better place
In the wrong hands it will decimate the human race.

Power of God

God is my light
And my might
He gives me peace to meet the night.
He gives me joy to meet the day
And courage to face any fray.
To meet the challenges which we all face
In the daily struggles of the human race.
To fight the good fight which we must,
If we are to be joined in the heavenly trust.

Temper

It comes on in a flash
Causing a man to crash
A feeling that stirs bad moods
And can lead to blood feuds

Its origin emanates from pride
Or factors that are not justified
It creates temporary insanity
And results in sudden calamity

It disturbs one's inner peace
And contaminates like grease
If one does not control its power
It can possess him and devour

Self-reflection can slow its wrath
And lead one down a calmer path
To overcome its pull
One needs a Godly rule.

The Addict

A prisoner of his addiction
He denies the truth as mere fiction.
Obsessed by his drug of choice
He ignores all rational voice.

Seeking to hide his shameful stain
His only goal is to numb the pain.
His loved ones beseech him to put down his syringe
But know without counselling he will continue to binge.

He hurts his kids and soon loses his wife
And is often short and angry with life.
He squanders his money to buy his next fix
And neglects his duties on his journey to Styx

To those who stand close he is hopeless and weak
To God made in his image he is incomplete.
He can only rescue himself once he chooses the good fight
To love himself again and reverse his downward flight

The Athlete

As the winter weather swirls outside, turmoil reigns within
Reminiscing on the memories of youthful days gone by.
Endless hours on the playgrounds and hardwood courts
Playing hard and free with a care for nothing but the game at hand.
Only the competition before me mattered,
Playing solely for the joy of the game.
Although the body's wear prevents the games from going on
The mind urges me to yet play and compete
As if the games did never end.
Creating a cruel dilemma for the athlete who cannot forget
Especially one who devoted such passion for the game.
Acceptance is the only balm
However inadequate it may be.

The Attack

Oh, God, what has happened to our lives
We were just eating honey from a beehive.
When without warning our village was overrun
By brutal men swarming us with machetes and guns.

They shot my gentle father in the head
And chopped my brother's body to shreds.
Oh, the horror was too much to bear
I fainted in anguish with a horrible stare.

When I awoke, I saw them spreading my mother's legs
And violating her body and soul in unspeakable ways.
She screamed with pain which was made worse by my witness
And struggled to survive the rapes with courageous fitness.

They burned our village without a care or thought
Enslaving my friends to men who sold and bought.
Miraculously, I escaped with the help of a boy
We ran into the tall grass seeking water and foy.

What makes these men so evil I will never know
They say it is because my religion was too low.
I was only a little girl who was always taught
To love the Lord and forgive those who fought.

I will never be the same as my life has been shattered
By prejudice, hate and evil things that cannot matter.
Oh, God, why did this happen to me and my kin
I was just a girl dreaming of school and soft skin.

I am now safe in a country which does not allow such a fight
And treats women and girls with respect and equal light.
Although I will never forget what I saw and endured
I know I am loved by my new friends and the Lord.

The Beach House

Scintillating beaches with white covered sand
Ever changing waves which retreat toward land.
Screeching gray seagulls gliding in flight
Searching for food to relieve their plight.

A school of dolphins passes smoothly over the waves
Causing those on the beach to express certain raves.
Two young lovers walking hand in hand on the beach
Their hearts and souls in touch and within reach.

Beach houses stand majestically overlooking the sea
Knowing the ocean's power could well set them free.
God is present and all around
Infusing blessings and warmth to this lazy sea town.

The tranquility and peace from such a place
Gives much pleasure and joy to the human race.

The Church

A sanctuary where the faithful pray
To examine ourselves and not betray
A place to seek that inner peace
To right our lives before the feast

Outwardly imperfect like its people
Innately holy under its steeple
Welcoming the wealthy and poor
Seeking to enrich those who want more

Started by our Lord who sought fellowship in his name
To bring his heavenly kingdom to earth without fame
With icons and incense to arouse our senses
And make us more humble and meek without fences

Within its walls we confess our sins
Seeking God's mercy and the ultimate win
To achieve glory and live above the Sanhedrin
The gospels teach us to love the least of our brethren.

The Elephant

Moving with grace despite bodies of size
The elephants walk slowly at sun rise.
With their young protected by the herd
Trumpeting love yet misunderstood.

To the poacher and hunter they see only gold
Shot without mercy, their bodies quiver and fold.
Coveted for their tusks they are given no chance
Against high-powered guns fired from a close stance.

Their death is a cruel blow to their orphaned babies left behind
Who panic in anguish at their dead mothers' bodies on their sides.
God knows the elephants feel the loss just as clear
As any human being who suffers death just as dear.

Without people of conscience these mammals will soon disappear
And earth shall mourn the passing of these
creatures with a grave tear.
Allowing greed and money to determine their fate
They will be lost forever with their most noble state.

A Friend

A person who accepts you as you are
And still raises you up like a bright star.
She accepts your vices and celebrates your strengths
And seeks to spend time with you at great lengths

She knows how you feel by just your sight
And is not afraid to be honest and risk a fight.
She is there to provide the warm light
When you encounter a long dark night

A good friend does not fear
To be with you when you shed a tear
The ultimate gift from above
Given to those who show their love

She encourages you to work hard to succeed
And provides support for you to lead.
There is nothing more valuable than a true friend
Far more precious than gold or any electronic trend

The Gambler

He plays for the thrill
Ignoring the bill.
The ultimate high is to beat odds that are stacked
While mesmerized by card decks that are packed.

An ace is respite to the gambler's bad luck
When it is paired with royalty that is struck.
The good streaks bring stakes that are daring and fast
But the tide quickly turns when the bad luck is cast.

The psyche of a gambler is innate and not learned
And can bring hardship and troubles for those who get burned.
Some cannot control their play and ruin their lives
For the presence of greed and excess are alive.

Casinos are a lure to the human faction
And prey on those who seek beauty and fast action.
A true gambler knows he will lose in dishonorable fashion
If he allows his good sense to succumb to his passion.

This pursuit of the money has brought many down
And made others depraved and full of deep frowns.
So beware of this vice which can tarnish the soul
And make wise men foolish and some lose their role.

The Godparent

A mentor who originates from the One above
Whose body and spirit encompass agape love.
A witness to your entry into the holy church
Who stands for you at baptism and throughout your time on earth.

A person who helps teach you right from wrong
And prevents you from being pressured from the throng.
Your conscience to help you discern true knowledge from the Lord
And to give you substance and peace to protect you from discord.

A godparent always has your back
And his prayers keep you on the right track.
To have such a person in your life
Is the greatest of blessings to keep you from strife.

The Good Steward

Some see a hungry man and say he is a bum
Others see the same poor soul and offer him their rum.
Some see a shivering child and close their eyes
While others wrap him in a blanket and hold him to the sky.

People rationalize their thoughts to justify their actions
Is it guilt, selfishness, or simple human reaction.
Yet our compassion is known by the God who cares
He recognizes and takes notice of how He fares

For remember, what you give to those in need
Will be yours forever when He takes heed.
Do not hide the things and talents which you possess
Share them instead to fill your heavenly chest.

Be a generous steward of His earthly gifts
And He will honor you with an eternal lift.

The Grandparents

Persons of great wisdom from a life of many years
Who have faced turmoil and overcome youth's fears.
The ones who take the time to listen to your story
And recognize the best in you and hold you up to glory.

Not hesitant to counsel you when you have gone astray
Or embrace and comfort you when your actions lead them to pray.
They understand your vices and protect you from that shame
When life presents adversity and temptations that are insane.

They share with you their true feel-
ings and express their ultimate delight
When you use your talents and time to do good for all to reunite.
They are loyal to a faith which has lasted
for over two thousand years
Knowing it will bring you joy in life and avoid immortal tears.

The Hero

A man whom all people revere
And elevate before their peers.
He is seen as brave and courageous
An idol for all times and ages.

Admired by persons of both sexes
He instills confidence and breaks down fences.
His swagger attracts women of all classes
And bestows awe and pride to the masses.

He is quite strong and invincible
And seeks to lead men of principle.
He protects the weak when subject to oppression
Yet despite his strength he is eager for confession.

He rides the white winged stallion of glory
And does not retreat when times get gory.
When the gates of heaven announce his arrival
The angels proclaim the good news of his revival.

The Immigrant

Living a life of hardship and strife
The foreign man seeks a better life.
Traveling with his family and sole possessions
He dreams of comfort in faraway mansions.

Hoping his children will be taught in fine schools
He employs his strong work ethic and plays by the rules.
Incessantly mocked for his color, customs and traits
He endures curses of derision and simmering hate.

Wop, Spic and dirty Greek the ignorant exclaim
Yet he maintains his composure and hides his disdain.
Determined to prevail he ignores chants to go home
Knowing in his heart he will no longer roam.

Despite hours of toil in dark smelly places
He discovers infinite joy in his family's faces.
When his children graduate with honors and a future of less pain
He beams with pride knowing his life was not spent in vain.

No longer hungry, cold and misplaced
He praises the Lord for his new found place.
The immigrant story is much of the key
To America's greatness and a land of the free.

The Journey

Born into a world of sin
We quickly bond with our kin.
We go to school to learn knowledge, wisdom, and rules
Making friends and acquiring the necessary tools.

Inspired by teachers who profess new thoughts
Yet we remain mired in doubt and a future of wrought.
From coaches who teach us valuable lessons of the day
We learn discipline, teamwork and the art of play.

Searching out partners whom we yearn to possess
Hoping they will fill our hearts with more and no less.
An innocent kiss or an intimate touch
Can easily lead to something special or not much.

We yearn to make a difference and be part of the cog
Yet fearing we will fall short, we remain immersed in thick fog.
Avoid drugs, bad characters, and excessive drink
For your future is bright and full of much link.

To those who work hard and persevere
Your mantle will rise with much revere.
Yet remember, fame and fortune are fleeting
As are beauty and youth.
Make the most of each day as you search for the truth.

Heed the advice of the wise men
Who live in accordance with the Ten.
For then you will remain faithful and do what is right
And the Lord will reward you with his peace and his light.

The Machine

An object which has changed and disrupted humankind
Making many of us obsessed, robotic, and so blind.
Upon waking we first reach for our phone
Before we pray or eat our morning scone.

It consumes every waking moment of our lives
Making us feel uneasy and restless like hives.
We have the need to look at it at every circumstance
Allowing this controlling machine to keep us in a trance.

We look at calls and emails which often are not new
And stare at videos and photos sent by who knows who.
Instead of talking with a person we text our thoughts and feelings
Permitting these toys to control us like some mechanic beings.

When we go out shopping for the latest fashion trends
Our cell phones are in use taking selfies with our friends.
We feel restless if we forget it or leave it far behind
And rush back to retrieve it so we do not miss a find.

Life was far more tranquil before this overbearing tool
Enabling us to enjoy quiet moments without its constant rule.
If we do not use this thing in a most judicious way
Our lives will pass before us with the beauty of each day.

The Miser

Possessed by gold and the love of money
He cannot focus on faith and honey.
Although he is taught to put the Lord first
His mind is occupied by purses that burst.

He goes through life seeking only more possessions
Incapable of tempering his material obsessions.
His soul is restless and black to the core
As he puts all his efforts on wanting more.

He ignores the pleas of those who seek help for the poor
And instead builds bigger barns to enrich his store.
Woe shall come to this sad and niggardly man
As he ages and hoards against God's command.

When called to account for his life and his things
He will cower in fear as the dark bells ring.
Heed the lessons of the prophets who warn of this fate
Be not like this rich man, share before it is too late.

The New Year Resolution

Promises and resolutions made by us all
We proclaim a new life, to make better calls.
Seeking to improve our faults and our vices
Less food, drink and gossip to avoid future crisis.

We will turn the other cheek and avoid all temptations
As we ask for absolution and embrace contemplation.
While visions of excess still ring in our heads
We seek a better life without too many meds.

Let the weak and meek forgo any goals
For we are determined and strong to meet our new roles
May we embrace our new promises as we move forward in time
So as not to forsake the Lord's blessings bestowed with such rhyme

Despite our weaknesses, we shall persevere
As we make a concerted effort to hold all in revere.
With love, peace and health to you all my friends,
We move forward with grace and sincere amends.

The Ocean

At its entry, the crashing waves
The ocean holds creatures in its bowels
Its depths tell the story of valiant souls
Lost at sea, silenced before their anointed time

Entombing the lives of colorful men
Seeking fame and riches in exotic ports
Some put to sea against their will
Gasping in holds with chains and stench

Whalers chasing monsters of the deep
Relentless, cruel and driven to death
Pirates searching for gold and treasure
Seeking to pillage a maiden voyage

Battleships laden with cannon balls
Galleys made up of enslaved men
Fearless, hopeless with desperate stares
Headed for graves of blood and water

In spite of the tales, the ocean yearns for more
Beckoning the oppressed and adventurous
Promising hope despite risk and peril
Fresh, uncertain and refusing to yield

Its tides never do cease
Its winds never blow out
Its secrets lay hidden
Forgotten, lost and free

The Player

Fixated by gyrating hips
Entranced by sensuous red lips.
The player surveys the field
Most conscious of those who yield.

A fast talker who makes women laugh
And who eyes those with a muscular calf.
His mannerisms are smooth seduction
And his approach is full of production.

His victims often have low self-esteem
And succumb to his insincere lines of steam.
Thinking they have found true love and affection
They are shattered when he departs after the session.

So be on guard for the player who raises you up
He may be the devil in disguise to sip your cup.
Flee from the gigolo with the cunning style
He will just bring sadness to your pretty smile.

The Self-Righteous

There was a man who thought he was good
People marveled at his image and for all he stood.
He attended church regularly and said the right things
Yet lavished himself with toys and elaborate rings.

He treated small men with the utmost disdain
Possessing a demeanor causing others much pain.
He was quick to judge his brother as lazy and sad
And considered himself special and others as cads.

His prayers were conceited and quick to denounce
The weak and the poor whom he sought only to trounce.
He sang false praises to the Lord on his road to hell
Yet considered himself worthy of a heavenly bell.

He gave only for show and to appease his pride
And did not hesitate to cheat and pass on a lie.
He was oblivious to the log in his own eye
Yet loved to point fingers at others who passed by.

His death was untimely and shocked those he knew
And he was carried off to judgment for a life most untrue.

The Terrorist

He claims to be a man of God
Yet commits sins with just a nod.
He often reveres a local Mullah
Believing he speaks for a God named Allah.

Five times daily he bows and prays to the East
Yet his actions are no better than a beast.
He subjugates women and despises free speech
Enslaving the wise men who attempt to teach.

He hates all who oppose him and do what is good
Confirming he is a man in an evil mood.
He forbids all debate and is quick with the sword
His actions from Satan, having fallen from the Lord.

He rapes women and children who come within his sight
Bringing suffering to a faith with higher might.
He raises his weapons to prove he is strong
Yet underneath his robes, his true nature is wrong.

Beseeching innocent children to cast aside their balls
And to join his lost crusade and follow his warped calls.
He convinces simple people to sacrifice their best
And brainwashes them to strap explosives on their chest.

Although he instills fear in the people of the West
His time on earth is dwindling and he'll soon be put to rest.

The Trees

Standing majestically like soldiers guarding a tomb
Withstanding the wind and snow with serenity and calm
They sway on mountain sides solemnly below the moon
Their roots firmly imbedded in the earth, in God's palm

The traveler seeks refuge under their branches
And rests beside the fire, the light singeing the night
Coyotes howl in the distance far from the ranches
While the grizzly protects its cub until dawn's light

The harsh gusts whisper through the pines
Remembering the days when the Indians danced below
They have passed as have the men who worked the mines
These trees have seen all kinds of times and fellows

Facing the blizzards with their bark
Fire and men threaten their existence
While they pay homage to God's mark
So tall, proud, mighty, and persistent

The Trial

Going to war for a cause
Putting life and leisure on pause
Skeptical if justice will prevail
Or if truth will be struck to no avail

The clients are anxious and out of sort
As lawyers argue nuances in court
When a witness receives an admonition
The jurors show their wary disposition

The evidence is weighed by dubious sighs
On faces disguising prejudicial eyes
The judge cautions the litigants to show respect
As the lawyers cower and are circumspect

The case is placed in the hands of the jury
As the clients are ready to show their fury
The verdict is read with a steady voice
As one side prepares to sing and rejoice

The Underdog

Living and performing with little expectation
He enters the arena with valid consternation.
In the back of his mind he hopes to be victorious
Yet his confidence is shaken by the more glorious.

All recall the ultimate conquest of the giant
By a young man who was brave and not compliant.
The one who refuses to back down and show fear
And instead is relentless in the midst of jeers.

For the crowds rejoice for the one who faces
Long odds and seeks redemption in strong places.
The people cheer for the lesser team
When it emits unexpected steam.

Victory is assured when the odds are overrun
Raising up the victor with admiration and fun.
Oh, David, how sweet is your rumble
When the mighty are made so humble.

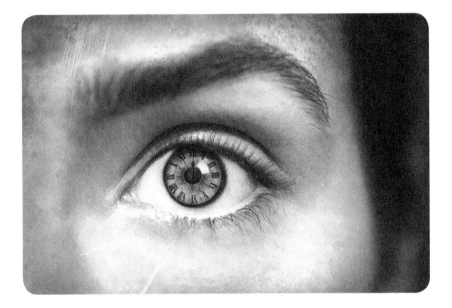

Time

That which cannot be conceived
Once gone it cannot be retrieved
It is quiet like space
Sparing no people or race.

It moves forward without pause
And gives hope to those with a cause.
It is merciful to those who suffer
And brings fond memories to the lover.

To a child it is more precious than sand
When a parent gives of herself and her hand.
Its gift is the ultimate sacrifice
To the lonely and forgotten in life.

The Lord will bestow his acclaim
To those who do not waste it in vain.
To use it with wisdom and discretion
Will ensure a life of value and confession.

To My Love

Life is fleeting
Your love is fair.
Life is exhilarating
Without a care.
To be there with you,
You are a dove in flight.
A beautiful sensation to behold
A memorable dark night.
You are passion and the light.

Worth

As I sit in contemplation
Seeking divine inspiration.
I wonder if I've lived a life of worth
Or squandered the gifts from God and earth

Have I used that which I have acquired
In a manner that God can admire.
Have I shared my talents
In ways that are gallant.

Or have I been selfish and self-consumed
Hoarding possessions for a future of doom.
Will I be proud come judgment day
Or sulk in fear of God's last say.

People rationalize their positions
In justifying more acquisitions
Yet the Gospels teach discipline and moderation
In living a life of purity and transformation

Sharing with others warm feelings
Sets the stage for honest dealings
It is never too late to change course
And live with meaning without remorse.

Beauty

It comes in shapes and colors of all kind
Arousing the hormones and the mind
Sometimes it appears in human form
Or as a rainbow after a storm

It can be found in spirit from within
The type of beauty that outlasts smooth skin
The shallow see only what is seen
The wise know it is holy and serene

Often found in nature or on the sea
It brings contentment without a fee
More common in a natural state
Some try to buy it to defy their fate

Possessed more often by those who are young
Sometimes taken for granted until it is flung
Some yearn for it as if it is supreme
Hoping to find it in some exotic cream

It manifests itself in flowers and trees
Opening the world around without keys
Those who are anxious and live imbalanced lives
Often are blind to that beauty which is alive

Rich and Poor

To live with need and desperation
In a world of dense population
Not being able to feed your family
Despite hours in the fields or factory

A condition of such helplessness
Amid color ads of happiness
A world of unjust inequality
Where some live so low and others so free

To billions a good meal is such a rare treat
To others it is just a piece of red meat
The rich isolate themselves from those who suffer
And enjoy such lives of luxury and buffer

They call the downtrodden lazy and sad
Oblivious to the lives they have had
Judging others without care or compassion
They ridicule those who seek fair ration

Ignoring the story of the rich man and Lazarus
They hoard their wealth and do not share their trust
Blind to the fact that their good fortune is a gift
Wanting more they become spiritually adrift

The Lord told us the poor would always be there
But he taught all people to be kind and to share
What is it that makes a rich person obsessed to want more
When he already has a good life and plenty to store

The Teacher

A mission of love, not merely a profession
The good teacher is a master of expression
She lends her soul to inspire those she teaches
To learn and see a world of new reaches

She is compassionate and kind
To help you develop your mind
She inspires with enthusiasm and grace
Her students feel the energy from her face

Her lessons stay with you until you die
Her memory enables you to fly
She gives a part of herself so you can grow
Teaching you to maximize and glow

She imparts both knowledge and class
So you can excel in life and surpass
She sees you and understands your feelings
And works hard to make learning so appealing

To have such a teacher is a blessing indeed
It gives you the courage and wisdom to succeed
In life you will meet those who will influence your ride
Few will impact you like the teacher who was by your side

A Father

A man who puts his family first
And does not flee at the time of birth
He knows that God has given him a precious gift
Ensuring that his wife and children have a lift

He is a person who works hard to provide
And must balance what to give and what to tithe
To his children, his time and attention are sought
Knowing true love and affection cannot be bought

He teaches his children honest love
By how he treats the woman he loves
He must exude kindness and discipline in his home
So his children see fairness and are less apt to roam

He is always willing to forgo his desires
To make sure his family has all they require
He puts the Lord first and is not afraid to pray
When his children need guidance and stray from the way

Noble fathers are found in all cultures and faiths
And are essential for success of the human race
One time a year we honor such a man
So vital to any prosperous clan

Marriage

The holiest of unions
God's gift of supreme fusion
Entered with optimism and hope
Mastered with compromise and scope

Resisting temptations which challenge its purity
Allowing holiness to perfect its security
Seeing another as no one has seen
Accepting their traits as cherished and sheen

Being able to show vulnerability
By showing forgiveness and humility
Treating your spouse with respect
Not fearful of being direct

Giving love in the presence of your kids
So they understand what the Lord bids
Being generous to those in need
Teaching your children to take the lead

A happy marriage is far greater than gold
And leads to a life more fulfilling, less cold
Since Abraham and Sarah this union has been hailed
Showing lovers how to co-exist and prevail

Aging

The youthful years pass with little concern
Until one realizes that there is no return
The energy dissipates as one grows older
Mortality is revealed as youth turns colder

Fond memories of the past give solace to those who age
Some yearn again for the glory of life's center stage
Thinking of precious time that was wasted in vain
Some turn to alcohol and drugs to ease their pain

The body becomes stiffer and less compliant
As routine movements become more reliant
Forgetting names and words becomes the norm
As one pauses to grasp this brewing storm

The body becomes wrinkled and loose to the touch
The taunt skin and muscles of youth replaced by a crutch
For some the abyss becomes total and complete
As loved ones are treated like strangers from the street

The fortunate will have their turn to become old
And to pass on their wisdom to those in their fold
If embraced by a family and loved ones who care
Then the journey to old age is less harsh to bear

Some turn to creams and lasers to delay their plight
Yet neither money nor status can turn back this fight
People of spirit and faith face this battle with hope
Knowing that the Lord's promise enables them to cope

The Jew

Papa why this yellow Star of David on our chests
And why are they yelling and treating us like pests.
What have we done to deserve such a fate
Banished from our homes and made to wait

These German soldiers with their dogs
Are robotic men lost in a fog
They are beating the Rabbi with vicious force
And stealing our possessions with no remorse

Oh Mama please stay close to my side
I am fearful of losing you on this train ride
It is dark and crowded and I cannot breathe
Where are we going without proper leave

When will this nightmare end
And our sweet lives begin again
Will we ever return home
Or be killed or made to roam

The train is coming to a halt, we have arrived
I hear dogs barking and see prisoners in line.
Why are they separating Papa and Sam
Please Mama don't let go of my hand

This camp smells so bad and why is it snowing
The chimneys are spewing things that are blowing.
Are we going to die in this evil and cold place
Or will God rescue his chosen people from this race

Exploitation

Existing in every place on earth
It stunts life and prevents renewed birth
Fueled by greed that taints the soul
It transforms men into trolls

Children and women often are pursued
And forced into slavery and servitude
Often placed in situations of horror
They become dead with no hope for tomorrow

Some are chained to oppressive sweltering shops
Others spend their hours in towering crops
Some are drugged and forced to perform tricks
For all kinds of men with swollen sticks

For money and diamonds, these men exploit
Without a care for the lives they destroy
Often, good people are aware of the scene
But do nothing to stop the evil or obscene

The only way to reverse the insanity
Is for righteous men to stop this calamity
If only we loved each other like brothers
Such evil in the world could be smothered

The Soldier

Entering the Armed Forces
with fervor and hope
With the goal of protecting
the weak with his stroke
Trained to fight and preserve
our nation's ideals
From aggressive men who
rape, burn and steal

Despite all his training
he is always exposed
And does not know when
he will encounter his foes
He endures hardship and
at times friendly fire
And despite his fears he
pretends not to tire

He ensures that his friends
are safe and secure
And watches their backs
so they too will endure
His encounters are sometimes
too much to bear
Yet his memories can lead
to death and despair

His family is proud but
concerned for his life
Praying for him to come
home intact to his wife
His experiences can
damage his mind
And make him fearful,
so different and blind

The emotional injury is
hidden from sight
And keeps him in anguish
and restless at night
He suffers from PTS
and has nightmares
He cannot forget what he
saw through his tears

His valor and fortitude
protect us from danger
His sacrifice is not always
known by the stranger
He appears in parades with
uniform and pomp
But often his life is as
stagnant as a swamp

For those men and women
who have served us all
Let us rejoice for their
lives and their call
Without them we would
be slaves of the evil
And live lives of darkness
with much upheaval

So be grateful to those who
have laid down their lives
They have sacrificed much
as known by their wives
To the men and women who
paid the ultimate price
We honor their memory
and supreme sacrifice

Victory

Reveled in our society as the ultimate high
It makes people delirious and prone to cry
Although hiding the shallowness of our existence
Holding up winning and excellence as consistence

Failing to realize that earthly victory is a sham
It obscures spirituality and God's gentle lamb
The weak see it as redemption for all that they lack
And seem to believe it will enhance their earthly pack

Inner victory is all that matters
To the holy man in humble tatters
For although the masses cheer with the mighty throng
Final peace belongs to the pure at heart, not the strong

Keep in perspective the victory on the field
It entertains you but does not provide the shield
Your life is not fulfilled with that win
For true happiness is found within

Multiple Sclerosis

It hits the young and middle age
Without warning its symptoms rage.
Overwhelming her joy and peace of mind
Afflicting the psyche and body most unkind

It cannot be seen by those around
Making it difficult to be found
When overheated it blurs the vision
Leading to helplessness and derision

It attacks the nerves with tingling and fire
Frustrating its victim and making her tire.
She mourns with a prayer at the loss of simple skills
Like buttoning her daughter's blouse without strong pills

When it heats up the spine she needs a cane
A previously healthy woman limping in pain
Bravely she walks with her head held high
Enduring the sad eyes of those who pass by

She yearns for the days when she was healthy and strong
Yet her faith in the Lord knows she has done no wrong.
She quietly accepts her disease
Knowing that someday she will be free

The Gentleman

He carries himself with peace and grace
While exuding class in making his case
He thinks before he speaks and prefers to hear
The perspective of others who teach without fear

He is a student of knowledge and things most rare
And defends the underdog and all that is fair
He lives a life of honor with positive thought
So his adversaries know he cannot be bought

He acquires only what he needs and does not hoard
For he understands his blessings come from the Lord.
He treats all people with respect and admiration
Knowing he cannot judge them without condemnation

He is invited to serve on boards of power
For he is a man who does not easily cower
Women look at him and see a fine catch
While men urge their daughters to be his match

Nostalgia

Those were the days they echo in our ears
Knowing full well we endured the same fears
The faded photos depict a life of all joy
Yet heartbreak was as common as a poor boy

Some live their lives by embracing the present
Others retreat to the past for their true crescent
Some seek out pleasure by seducing young faces
Others search for peace in long ago places

Remembering our past as carefree and grand
Dancing and drinking to the classic rock bands
The Stones, Dillon and Zeppelin were all the rage
As we partied with pleasure on life's center stage

Feeling quite stoned as we shared a toke in the lair
We were young and invincible with a thick head of hair
The girls all around were steamy as the night
Blinded by our hormones, we savored that sight

Those days are all gone as the years have flown by
Bringing no solace to the dreamer or truth to the lie

The Lawyer

Despised by many
Yet envied by all
Protecting his client in arguing his call
A good lawyer is willing to accept the fall

He worries and weeps for the people he feeds
Not knowing if his skill will fulfill their needs
He carefully listens in court
To provide strength to his retort

Woe to him who is weak
Or knows not how to speak
Silence is sometimes the balm
To help fortify the calm

His skills are essential
To give his case potential
He cares more than you think
To bring justice to the rink

The Life and Times of Alexander Veronis

Born of Greek immigrants from the island of Crete
They sought out the country with gold in the streets
Allen was the fourth son of six children born during their climb
While his father toiled in foul smelling factories in difficult times

Nicholas and Anna struggled to provide for their brood
And work as a furrier put Nicholas in a somber mood
During the depression they swallowed their pride
And sought help from the government while Anna cried

With hard work and incessant prayers by Anna to the Lord
Their situation improved and their dreams were restored
Anna encouraged her children to be all they could be
Telling them to seek knowledge and keep the faith of the three

While his brothers Peter and George fought the Japs on the seas
Allen and his siblings worked hard for their college degrees
His mother prayed for the safe return of her boys
When her sons returned home, she praised God with great joy

Anna wanted her son Allen to be a Greek Orthodox priest
In honor of the Lord who kept her sons safe from the beast
Allen attended Lafayette College with the
help of John, his kind brother
While his mother taught them to be faith-
ful and to love one another

Allen went to the seminary and was inspired to serve
The least of his brethren with courage and verve
He fell in love with a woman named Pearl from Asbury Park
Who came from a Greek clan which was tough with much spark

Soon after, Allen and Pearl travelled to Greece
To master the language and seek youthful peace
Hard work was interrupted by moments of love
Resulting in healthy sons, two gifts from above

Sent by a bishop to serve a town surrounded by farms
They encountered God fearing people who had so much charm
The young priest and his wife started their Christian mission
And flourished with parishioners with similar volition

Father Veronis and Presbytera Pearl have a noble vision
Encouraging their flock to be generous without division
They have welcomed all races to share the Orthodox way
And have spread the gospel with fervent passion and sway

Through example, Father V has taught his people to give
Of their talents, words and money so they could truly live
He has admired those who love the faith and the church
And those who seek to develop their spiritual search

He spreads the gospel to all nations
And promotes international relations
He supports mission priests in Africa and around the globe
Pushing the Orthodox church to embrace a similar robe

Father Alex is an exceptional leader
Who can still chant in Byzantine meter
He has inspired many to attend the seminary
And give their lives to God and the Virgin Mary

He loves to mingle with his people
And spend time under his steeple
He has pitched at the church picnic well into his eighties
And imparts wisdom to his bible study of older ladies

He has been a leader of the youth and took them to the shore
Teaching them to be good Christians with values and rapport
The youth of the 70s and 80s will never forget his leadership
Which was boundless and upbeat with so much fellowship

He can preach with the best and give relevant talks
Of love and forgiveness without any balks
On Good Friday he would dress like a disciple or sage
And recount a tale of Christ's love in the Biblical age

His wife Pearl has become a jewel in her time
Enabling his ministry to reach a deeper rhyme
She has ministered with great love and compassion
And soothes the lonely and poor in gentle fashion

She has complemented his mission and preaching
With kindness, enthusiasm and wise teaching
They have raised five children with so much love
Instilling in them Biblical lessons from above

During times of turmoil and hate
He promotes reconciliation without debate
He loves people of all nations and color
And opens the church to them like no other

He has sought to eradicate hunger on earth
And to fill every belly regardless of birth
He led the CROP walk for 40 plus years
Raising millions for those starving with fear

Well into his 80s, he has continued serving the Lord
Giving hope to the hopeless and those who've been gored
He helps the forgotten and those languishing in prison
And counsels them on a new life of hope with vision

Father Veronis has never lost sight of his heavenly union
Seeking the Lord he has served faithfully with communion
He continues to fight the good fight and
will someday finish the race
Having always done what was right in his time and his place.

Pearl (Kacandes) Veronis

Born to parents from the Greek mountains of the ancient Gods
    She has charisma and charm like a prophet with his rod
    Her parents immigrated to America to seek a better life
For Pearl and her three brothers in a land with less strife

    They settled in Neptune, a town close to the sea
    And her father George tended bar for modest fees
Speaking no English, her mother Chrysoula yearned for Greece
And cried daily for her homeland and her weaves full of fleece

With her young children in tow, she returned to visit her village
Not knowing the Germans would soon conquer Greece and pillage
    Pearl witnessed her grandparents perish from famine
    And lost her animals and innocence to German cannon

She ran messages for the Greek guerillas with very little fear
But was caught and made to witness death through bitter tears
    Her brothers were scattered all over Greece trying to survive
    While George's repeated attempts to help were denied

    Miraculously, her family endured the World War ordeal
    And were reunited to their father by a mighty ship's keel
Because of their lack of English, they were placed in the wrong class
Never forgetting their animals while sending back packages of grass

With hard work and perseverance they learned to read and write
    And excelled in high school and sports with an occasional fight
    With the help of her older brother John, Pearl attended Clark U
And graduated with a degree in teaching and a life that was true

Despite her mothers' great desire for her to marry a man of wealth
She fell in love with a seminarian with some degree of stealth
They met near the surf where his father had a small shop
And courted in earnest until they were ready to drop

From that day on Allen went to the beach
Searching for Pearl who was getting ready to teach
Chrysoula did not want her daughter to marry an Orthodox priest
She dreamed instead of a lawyer or doctor with a grand feast

Soon however she grew to love this man who was the one
Who would make Pearl happy before the setting of the sun
They had a traditional Greek wedding in Asbury Park
Where the family's celebration made quite the mark

Soon after, they flew off to Athens and lived in a simple place
With Tom and his wife Vaso who were running the same race
The couples were romantic and had three baby boys
So Niko, Jimmy and George played with the same toys

Allen perfected his Greek and grew a beard in place of his stubble
And Tom followed suit with a black beard
that looked much like a double
Upon graduation, Allen was assigned to
a church in a small PA town
They thought it was a stepping stone for a future cathedral so round

Soon they discovered beautiful people who loved life and the Lord
And decided to make their lives here and buy a car made from Ford
With Allen's great passion and Pearl's attractive young face
Pearl bore two more children whom she dressed in fine lace

They have always been generous to the poor and the oppressed
Even bringing home a young girl who lived a life of distress
Pearl treated her new daughter Kitty like one of the gang
Teaching her values and sharing the siblings' orange Tang

They have a special heart for those who spread the gospel
And Allen and Pearl challenge hate spread by the hostile
Opening up their home to people of all races
They share all they have with many colored faces

They have carried out a ministry of compassion and light
Leading parishioners who love them and do what is right
Pearl taught in the Sunday school and passed on her knowledge
To young children who listened in awe before going off to college

All her life, Pearl has visited the lonely and the old
Reminding them they are still a vital part of the fold
She loves life and people and can talk with the best
Mesmerizing the listener to feel as good as the rest

She always kisses people and anything that moves
And never leaves a person empty, bitter or rude.
She has truly been a pearl hanging from a gold cord
And she has lived a full life connected to the Lord

Biography of
Nicholas A. Veronis

Nicholas was born in 1960 in Athens, Greece. His is the eldest son of a Greek Orthodox priest, Alexander Veronis, who has had a fifty-five year ministry in Lancaster, Pennsylvania.

Nicholas, known by his friends as Niko, graduated from Lafayette College in 1982 and the University of Pittsburgh School of law in 1986. He and his partner, James Hagelgans started the law firm of Hagelgans & Veronis in 1994. He and his firm only represent the underdogs in legal cases again corporations and insurance companies.

He and his partner are involved in philanthropy in their community, local theater and sponsor scholarships for local graduating seniors each year through the Martin Luther King Scholarship fund. They have created an Endowment for Orthodox Missions. They are supportive of their churches and involved in helping the less fortunate of society. Niko and his wife Susan are members of Leadership 100 of the Greek Orthodox Church.

Niko has served as President of his church and on the church council for over thirty years. His interests include reading, writing, international affairs, Eagles football, biking, animals, poetry, inspirational movies and spiritual enhancement. He has been married to Susan Veronis, a former teacher, for thirty years. He and his wife have a daughter, Rachel, who is a teacher in Philadelphia and son, Nikitas, a recent graduate of Temple University.

CPSIA information can be obtained
at www.ICGtesting.com
Printed in the USA
BVOW10s1245120817
491792BV00006B/9/P